MODELING GOD

MODELING GOD

Religious Education for Tomorrow

by
Gloria Durka
and
Joanmarie Smith

PAULIST PRESS
New York / Paramus / Toronto

Library of Congress
Catalog Card Number: 75-44595

ISBN: 0-8091-1933-1

Published by Paulist Press
Editorial Office: 1865 Broadway, N.Y., N.Y. 10023
Business Office: 400 Sette Drive, Paramus, N.J. 07652

Printed and bound in the
United States of America

Contents

*To Jack McCall
with gratitude and affection*

ACKNOWLEDGMENTS

Much of the reflection here presented was made possible by the stimulation provided by the work of process thinkers in philosophy, theology and educa tion. Their lectures and conversations encouraged us to further pursue the topic chosen for this study.

Grateful acknowledgment is made to our close colleagues who guided our work from its initial inception to its final form. Their useful criticism and encouragement assisted us in many incalculable ways, especially through their detailed comments on the content and structure of the study.

In addition to the immediate research done for this study, this work has grown out of many theological discussions through the years, and we are grateful to all our colleagues and students who have encouraged us and contributed to our thinking. The responsibility for the positions taken here is, of course, our own.

1
Modeling Reality

What we will be proposing in this chapter is that faith is the fundamental category of existence. It is the condition of our human interaction with all of reality What we call knowing is actually a form of believing. One can easily imagine the ramifications such a position would have in the whole of life. We will, however, confine our explorations in future chapters to the key areas of theology and education.

Most of us are aware that the major decisions in our lives are based on faith. We realize that we can never know, in the sense of having certitude, that our choice of career, marriage partner or place to live, for example, is the best choice. We are aware, therefore, after the slightest reflection, that the shape our lives take is basically the result of believing. What we believe is an interpretation of reality that seems to make the most sense of our experience. That one has talents to be a good doctor, that a prospective spouse would provide lifelong happiness, that living in New Mexico would be more satisfying than living in New York are typical of the interpretations to which we are referring. One accepts the possibility of these interpretations being modified or even scrapped as others seem to make even better sense. In other words, one recognizes that beliefs, without which one cannot act at all, are quite tentative.

1

While readily acceding to the major role of belief in our lives we are inclined to distinguish between it and "cold hard facts." By facts we usually mean some indisputable information about reality. Our grasp of facts is termed knowledge. We are going to argue that so-called facts are also simply interpretations of phenomena in which many, perhaps a majority of persons, believe. If there are any facts in the accepted sense of the term mentioned previously, they are so trivial as to be almost negligible. They might be along the lines of the exact wording of a particular poem. Concerning the more significant information of why it was written or what it means, the poet himself can only give his beliefs.

A well-worn example of a fact that dissolves into interpretation is "Columbus discovered America in 1492." Speculations about the prior arrival in the New World of Asians or Vikings are not the issue here. Examine the fact as it is. The year 1492 is a Gregorian interpretation of time not even operative when Columbus landed in San Salvador. America is now a term chauvinistically appropriated by citizens of the United States. Upon meeting someone in Europe who claimed to be an American and then further identified himself as being from San Salvador, who would not be taken aback? So it is with "discover." We are at present loath to bestow the term "discoverer" on someone who incorrectly identifies what he or she has found. What we will be suggesting throughout is that the most literal statements turn out to be metaphors.

At this point we would like to substitute the term "model" for what we have been describing as an interpretation of reality. Although "world-view" or "hypothesis" could have also been used, we hope by an analysis of the use of "model" to trace historically the evolution of our thesis that faith is the condition of our human interaction with reality. We will rely for the most part on the findings of the sciences which, by definition, claim knowledge in the sense of indisputable information as the note that distinguishes them from the other disciplines. If there were/are significant "facts" they must certainly be the province of the sciences. It might be wise at this point to provide at least a working definition of reality. Let it mean at this stage of our argument a quality of phenomena that exists independently of our perception of desire.

The Meaning of Models

"Model" as used in conversation has a number of related references. It can mean a scaled replica of a larger entity such as a model airplane, or a replica of something yet to be constructed—an office complex, for example, or a city. It can also mean a sample. Men and women from modeling agencies display samples of merchandise for our edification and are themselves supposed to represent examples of those who can buy the product. Models may also refer to embodiments of an ideal. When we speak of model students or model marriages we use the term in this last sense.

Linguistic images might be called verbal models. Speaking figuratively in simile or metaphor, one tries to represent experience in imaginative and novel terms. As used in the sciences, a model has been described as "a structure of symbols and operating rules which is supposed to match a set of relevant points in an existing structure or process."[1]

Purposes of Models

In all the uses of "model" that have been cited, the term is employed to clarify, illuminate and vivify a phenomenon whether it is a personality or a situation. Implied in all these usages is the assumption that one has access to the original reality against which one may evaluate the accuracy of its model. This assumption is the basis of a theory of knowledge called realism which contends that the world is pretty much as we perceive it. Probably few persons would maintain the simplicity of this position. On the other hand, most of us operate with the conviction that reality is accessible and that some people know it as it is and share the information with us. These persons are most likely to be physical scientists. Lately, however, considerable doubt has been cast upon even this posture.

Almost imperceptibly a newer meaning of "model" has entered our thinking, a meaning whose implications have yet to be fully explored. "Model" has come to refer to a purely mental construct which makes no claim to a point-for-point correspondence to reality, and which is sustained by conversation more than by experiment. Models in this sense appear to be like the projections of mathematicians, or perhaps more accurately like the analogies used in God-talk by traditional theologians. Analogous statements made by theologians never claimed to give any hard information about the Other. "Model" here seems to resemble myth if we mean by myth an earlier people's attempt to construct an explanation of their experience. It is interesting to note that as models have relinquished their claim to a point-for-point reference to reality, myths, once considered primitive fictions, are engaging scholars as less and less far-fetched.

In any case, it becomes obvious that a totally different theory of knowledge must underpin this shift in the use of "model." It is a theory suggesting that perhaps these models are the only access we have to reality, and that perhaps the best we can do is to construct less and less inappropriate models.

Tracing the Shift

This relatively novel use of "model" was a long time coming into being. It is not a little threatening.

Travelers, whether in the service of commerce or their country's conquering spirit, have always come across models of government, religion and family life other than their own. The trauma or at least the questioning that this experience might occasion was neutralized by the studied conviction of the travelers that their home-based models were the true ones. These others were the corruptions and distortions attributable to the primitive or ignorant mind. It is a commonplace of history that conquering nations benevolently attempted to educate their conquests to the true religion, best form of government, true family life, and so on, through all the institutions.

More recently, as the revolution in transportation and communication made the experience of other peoples' styles of existence immediate, the attempt to retain one's own world-view as the standard against which all others are to be evaluated has taken the form of apologetics-like rhetoric or the use of political pressure. The Catholic Church in the earliest stages of this now truly pluralistic society took great pains to educate its adherents in arguments which demonstrated that it alone possessed the truth. Nations went to similar pains to reinforce the idea that their particular governmental and economic structures represented the acme of political insight. Those who refused to be persuaded were accurately labeled "dangerous subversives" and prevented from promulgating their ideas when they were not imprisoned outright.

The contemporary scene is "awkward." The ecumenical movement which can be said to obtain among nations as well as among religions has placed us in the position of accepting differences as valid while at the same time trying to maintain one's own experience as in some way more valid. The bind in which we find ourselves can surely be ascribed to the little attention that has been paid to working out a theory of knowledge which could underpin pluralism. In the vacuum created by this lack of study, young people are operating on just that notion of relativism former generations justifiably dreaded and tried to forestall. It almost seems as if those who do not think there is one true model of everything think every model is as good as every other one. The latter position is as simplistic as the former and certainly equally as dangerous. In a world where no viewpoint is better than another, all education becomes superfluous. Such a world is irrational. Choice becomes a matter of taste and there is no accounting for taste.

History of the New Skepticism

Skepticism has been a viable attitude toward the possibility of knowledge in the usual sense since the time of the Sophists. Gorgias, a fourth century B.C. proponent of skepticism, formulated the position in its most extreme form: "There is no reality. And if there were we could not know it. And if we could know it we could not communicate it to others." Protagoras' dictum that "man is the measure of all things" is a less satirical embodiment of a theory of knowledge propagated in Socratic times. Socrates' life work might be characterized as the successful attempt to disabuse his listeners of this cynical attitude toward the character of what we know when we know. The realistic position (we can and do know reality as it is) of Plato and later of Aristotle has informed Western thinking until only recently. There have always been, of course, philosophers who took issue with the perennial notion of knowing but never with too much influence on the proverbial "man-in-the-street."

The first telling chinks in the realist's position might be traced to the late 1800's when the newly formed science of psychology began to accumulate evidence of the subjective input of perception. Sensation as we experience it reflects the make-up of the receptors—our eyes, ears, skin—more than the stimuli itself. Apparently color as we see it is in the eyes, sound in the ear, taste in the taste buds and olfactory sense. More recent studies have established that certain tactile nerve endings will send the message "hot" or "cold" to the brain (depending on their location on the skin) regardless of whether the applied stimulus is hot or cold. Such evidence has made it increasingly difficult to maintain the position that we know reality as it is.

Another psychological phenomenon, of which we have always been instinctively aware but is now being scientifically documented, is also contributing to the difficulty of the realist's view. Robert Rosenthal has called his findings "The Pygmalion Effect." It is a commonplace of our experience that other persons "shape up" to the shape of them that we project. Rosenthal has statistically validated what has been a basic theme in literature from the myth of Galatea to Don Quixote's Dulcinea. Working with classes of children having comparable backgrounds and IQ's he established that the students realize their teacher's models of them. This suggests that far from models merely reflecting, they may *effect* reality—create what we experience even more dramatically than our sense receptors.

Another newly established discipline, the sociology of knowledge, began to make similar allegations about the hard-nosed quality of reality almost simultaneously with the psychologists. Max Scheler, a philosopher, coined the phrase "sociology of knowledge" in the 1920's. The sociologists who have explored and compared "reality" and the knowledge of it through history and myriad cultures are unanimous: our institutions, whether we speak of marriage, child-rearing, political organization of a nation or religion, are simply constructs of society.

Whether or not some social constructs better approximate the really-real than others is outside the province of sociologists. They simply observe and record their observations. They observe that a "reality" lasts only as long as people accept it as such, after which it is frequently replaced by an opposite "reality."

We have been able to absorb the suggestions of the social scientists that apparently reality is neither so accessible nor the way we perceive it because we have been persuaded that at least the physical sciences were with increasing speed revealing the secrets of nature. In fact, we have used the physical sciences as the criteria of the real according to which we acknowledge that we do not, for example, perceive light or sound as it is.

It has been quite disconcerting, therefore, to learn from contemporary historians of science that the physical sciences do not claim direct access to reality either. It has become more and more obvious, for example, as we explore the atomic and sub-atomic dimensions of our universe, that the nature of our findings more accurately reflects our hypotheses and the nature of the instruments of research than the universe itself. Like our senses which deliver the world to us according to their construction, so do the instruments of science yield information according to their construction.

Perhaps more to the point, the historians of science are now suggesting that scientific theories are simply models which more or less successfully mediate our interactions with nature. Whether or not the atom is in any way like the representations of it in science textbooks is unknown and perhaps unknowable. In any case it is not especially pertinent. The model as we have it is a fertile thesis.

The work that most popularized this realization is Thomas Kuhn's *The Structure of Scientific Revolutions*. Speaking of the problems of historians, Kuhn admits that they confront "growing difficulties in distinguishing the 'scientific' component of past observation and belief from what their predecessors had readily labeled "error" and "superstition." The more carefully they study, say, Aristotelian dynamics, phlogistic chemistry, or caloric thermodynamics, the more certain they feel that those once current views of nature were, as a whole, neither less scientific nor more the product of human idiosyncracy than those current today."[2] The studies of scholars seem to set in relief the role of imagination and faith in the great scientific breakthroughs, rather than the studied observation, hypothesis and validation we have so long associated with the scientific method. This conclusion is reinforced by the fact that Copernicus' theory was not more accurate than Ptolemy's and did not lead directly to any improvement in the calendar. Again, the wave theory, after it was first announced, was for some years not even as successful as its corpuscular rival in resolving the problems in optics at that time.[3] Such incidents in the history of science cause Kuhn to continue:

The man who embraces a new paradigm at an early stage must often do so in defiance of the evidence provided by problem-solving. He must, that is, have faith that the new paradigm will succeed with the many large problems that confront it, knowing only that the older paradigm had failed with a few. A decision of that kind can only be made on faith.[4]

In sum, the theories of the physical sciences begin to resemble more and more the projections of mathematicians with all the difficulties they entail. Peter Berger has expressed the dilemma most aptly: "Without a doubt mathematics is a projection of certain structures of human consciousness. Yet the most amazing fact about modern science is that these structures have turned out to correspond to something 'out there.' Mathematicians, physical scientists and philosophers of science are still trying hard to understand just how this is possible."[5]

Some thinkers would submit as a solution that reality is infinitely malleable, conforming itself with equal validation to the model believed in. Studies in para-psychology which are being taken more and more seriously have contributed to this view of the roles of models. A typical example of what we mean might be the comparison of the "fact" that in the world model of the typical Western scientific man fire burns. Yet there are well-documented instances of hundreds, even thousands of religiously inspired persons walking through fires registering 1328°F. in Ceylon. Apparently so basic a belief that fire burns is just that—a belief constitutive of the findings. It may be that reality is so variegated, so rich that it will shape itself to any model proposed to it much like any container dipped into the sea will find the water taking its shape. This may or may not be a valid metaphysical conclusion. In any case it is unnecessary to explore that thesis in this essay. We are simply concerned to establish that the models we project are the condition of our experience, that our experience reflects these models and that knowledge is faith that our use of these models will somehow be vindicated.

A Theory of Knowledge

Certain elements of a model theory of knowledge which would make the most sense of the points outlined present themselves immediately. Although we have taken the sciences as the focus of our examination, it has, we hope, become evident that rather than the scientific method being esoterically distinct from math, the humanities and the arts, the approach is quite similar. Literature, like paintings, is judged by its continuing capacity to deliver and fertilize our experience. This now seems to be what we expect of our scientific theories. We should not be surprised, therefore, to hear Einstein saying, "When I examine myself and my methods of thought I come to the conclusion that the gift of fantasy has meant more to me than my talent for absorbing positive knowledge."[6]

Knowing then seems accurately described as the constructing of believable models. American philosophy in the first half of the twentieth century proposed an epistemology most consonant with our conclusion that knowledge cannot be regarded as the result of passive receptivity.

Knowledge or science is a work of art, and, like any work of art, confers upon things traits and potentialities which did not *previously* belong to them. Objection from the side of alleged realism to this statement springs from a confusion of tenses. Knowledge is not a distortion or perversion which confers upon its subject matter traits which *do* not belong to it, but is an act which confers upon non-cognitive material traits which *did* not belong to it. It marks a change by which physical events exhibiting properties of mechanical energy, connected by relations of push and pull, hitting, rebounding, splitting and consolidating, realize characters, meanings and relations of meanings hitherto not possessed by them. Architecture does not add to stone and wood something which does not belong to them, but it does add to them properties and efficacies which they did not possess in their earlier states. It adds them by means of engaging them in new modes of interaction having a new order of consequences.[7]

In emphasizing the active or constructive nature of knowing, these philosophers did not seem to stress the role of the model or expectation according to which the construction took place. It is this element that we are stressing. Implicit in every doing is a model of what one is doing—of what one is going to discover or know as a result. This appears to conform to the classic model of science: hypothesis, experiment, validation. It differs from the classical view of science because it claims that all you have at the end is an hypothesis that works, not reality itself. Or, as phrased at the beginning of this chapter, hypotheses or models are the only access we have to reality.

Aesthetic Criteria

Undoubtedly, the most problematic feature of any notion of knowledge that emphasizes the elements of imagination and faith is the danger of relativism that it seems to presuppose. We submit that one model is not necessarily as good as another and that the criteria for judging one model over against another are, in the final analysis, aesthetic.

This is not to say there is no place for validation as it is usually meant. Let us take an almost inane example. One rarely says in passing, "It is raining." To do so would be akin to a sneeze—a simple organic reaction to irritating stimuli. One usually means something else by the statement, such as: "Wear your rubbers." "The picnic is off." "Our prayers have been answered." The meaning, or interpretation, or model implicit in the statement is obviously an hypothesis yet to be warranted. The simple statement that "it is raining," however, is part of the trivia that can pass for facts which we mentioned earlier. It represents a rather un-nuanced convention that most people accept as symbolizing a state of weather. Whether it is the best way to symbolize a state of affairs, that is, whether it would be less inaccurate to say there is precipitation due to increased condensation of cloud moisture, is beside the point here. What is at issue is that while one may not be able to phrase the best interpretation of the weather conditions, one can at least establish, usually by observation, that it is or is not raining. The point: the proposition "It is raining" is not as good as "It is not raining"—especially if it is not raining! It seems that a principle can be inferred from the discussion so far: the more insignificant a proposition is the more easy it is to establish, at least when it is false.

As soon as one moves into the significant—and here we refer to the meaningful in the sense of making a difference—other criteria obtain. Later we will refer to the most significant models as life-defining models. If, as we suggested above, when you say "It is raining" you are really making other points, the principle of empirical validation is no longer readily applicable. "Wear your rubbers" probably contains any or all of a whole spectrum of models: "Wet feet cause colds." "Your shoes will be ruined." "Wet shoes are uncomfortable." Most researchers into the common cold would denounce the first as an old wives' tale at the moment, although most of them would not be surprised if further research reinstated the wives' tale as the very latest medical findings some years hence. That one's shoes will be ruined is another of those relatively insignificant beliefs that might easily if expensively be verified or falsified. On the other hand it is impossible to know if one should have called off the picnic. Even if one did not and a good time was had by all, there is no way to demonstrate with certitude that a better time would not have been had at a postponed picnic. As one comes to the most comprehensive and significant of the possible implications of the "rain," we are in the realm of momentous hypotheses whether of religion, science or politics. Empirical evidence can make one's belief more and more plausible but never prove it beyond dispute.

At this point we are proposing that aesthetic criteria be employed in the judgment of competing models. Since we have based so much of our argument on the present state of science, it is pertinent to quote Kuhn again:

> Something must make at least a few scientists feel that the new proposal is on the right track, and sometimes it is only personal and inarticulate aesthetic considerations that can do that. Men have been converted by them at times when most of the articulable technical arguments pointed the other way. When first introduced, neither Copernicus' astronomical theory nor De Broglie's theory of matter had many other significant grounds of appeal. Even today Einstein's general theory attracts men principally on aesthetic grounds, an appeal that few people outside of mathematics have been able to feel.[8]

We suggest that similar considerations are appropriate in determining significant commitment to any model. However, we do not think the criteria are so personal or inarticulable as Kuhn does, John Dewey referred to the existence of a tertiary quality of a situation which makes it this or that particular event. Dewey takes his lead from our disposition to refer to paintings as having a Titian quality, for example. No particular aspect of the canvas merits the description. It is rather an overriding and organizing mode of connections that figuratively colors the work, making it a Titian.

A quality is considered aesthetic when it converts brute existence into meaningful relationships that yield a consummatory experience. A model may

be considered to have aesthetic quality when the constituent elements acquire an enhanced existence because of their participation in the whole. There is, in
addition, what Dewey calls an elegance in the inevi-
table logic with which these disparate parts constitute the whole. Furthermore, the most significant
models will be characterized by the unpredictable,
the spontaneous, the not yet formulable and the ineffable. Paradoxically, while embodying an interpretation of experience that calls forth awe even con-
templation—the truly significant model will also be
instrumental. It will suggest even as it stands the possible generation of more nuanced, more comprehensive models.

In these next chapters we hope to demonstrate
the difference it makes when one claims only to have
models of reality and to utilize the criteria we have
set out for submitting one or more particular models
in education and theology as superior to others.

Study Guide

1. The authors contend that "knowing is also a form
   of believing."

   We readily admit that we make many major decisions on the basis of "faith." Yet we often define
   knowledge of reality as a clear grasp of life's cer-
   tainties. What role does interpretation play in the
   apprehension of "hard, cold facts."

2. In order to describe knowledge in a more functional way, the authors substitute the term "model" for our way of interpreting reality. They suggest further that the meaning of this term has begun to change in a way which may be somewhat frightening.

   A. In conversation we use the term "model" when we wish to deal more practically with some original reality. What do we imply in speaking of "a model car," "a floor model," "a model family"?

   B. This work suggests that the meaning and purpose of the term "model" is beginning to change. Model has come to refer "to a purely mental construct which makes no claim to point-for-point correspondence with reality." What is meant by the term "mental construct"? Give examples of "mental constructs" we use to facilitate our work without giving much thought to the reality they represent.

   C. In using myths to illustrate our ideas, what attitude do we take to their point of correspondence with reality (historical and geographical facts, for example).

3. Underlying the change in the way we use models today is a gradual shift away from "realism," the theory of knowledge that contends that the world is pretty much as we perceive it.

   A. How has the revolution in travel and communications challenged our assumptions that our models of government, family and religion are the "true" ones?

B. How has young people's widening experience of different beliefs led them to operate on the basis of relativism? Does acceptance of the cliché that "one idea is as good as another" affect the quality of any of our routine daily choices (selection of the evening's news program, the weekly magazine, the breakfast cereal)?

C. How has the science of psychology weakened the realist's position?

D. The social scientists tell us that reality is neither "so accessible or the way we perceive it." Give examples. Why do we accept their contentions so easily?

E. For many of us the physical sciences are the last discipline likely to yield the claim of access to real facts. How have contemporary historians of science and the physical sciences challenged this assumption?

4. The authors tell us that the models we construct may be our only access to reality, "that the models we project are the condition of experience." What role does our "model" of reality play in our perception of (a) the "true" character of a juvenile delinquent, (b) the personality of a two year old child?

5. This work proposes that "knowing seems accu-

rately described as the constructing of believable models."

A. In what way does this theory differ from the classical model of science: hypothesis, experiment, validation?

B. How does it differ from the relativist position?

6. To distinguish between models the authors suggest that we use aesthetic criteria: "A model may be considered to have aesthetic quality when the constituent elements acquire an enhanced existence because of their participation in the whole."

A. How do the authors apply this definition to a painting by Titian?

B. In what way might our "model" of a desirable renovation project affect our way of perceiving a brownstone house in the area to be renewed?

Readings

For an overview of American process thought, including aesthetics, see:

Dewey, John. *Experience and Nature*. New York: Dover Publications, 1958.

On models in the sciences, see:

Berger, Peter and Thomas Luckmann. *The Social*

Construction of Reality. New York: Doubleday & Co., 1966.

Kuhn, Thomas. *The Structure of Scientific Revolutions* (second edition). Chicago: University of Chicago Press, 1970.

Notes

1. Karl Deutsch, "On Communications Models in the Social Sciences," *Public Opinion Quarterly*, Fall 1952, p. 357.

2. Thomas Kuhn, *The Structure of Scientific Revolutions*, 2nd edition (Chicago: University of Chicago Press, 1970), p. 2.

3. *Ibid.*, p. 154.

4. *Ibid.*, p. 158.

5. Peter Berger, *The Sacred Canopy* (New York: Doubleday, 1967), p. 181.

6. Ronald W. Clark, *Einstein* (New York: World Publishing Co., 1971), p. 86.

7. John Dewey, *Experience and Nature* (New York: Dover Publications, 1958), p. 154.

8. Thomas Kuhn, *op. cit.*

2
Education after Modeling

We have tried to demonstrate that implicit in every statement about reality or any aspect of it is a theory of knowledge. We have, in addition, attempted to explicate a theory of knowledge consonant with the contemporary findings of various disciplines, especially science. In this theory knowledge is indistinguishable from belief. Our efforts have not been addressed to this or that theory in a particular subject area but rather to the effect such a view of knowledge has with regard to life-defining models.

If faith is the condition of our human interaction with reality, then education can be spoken of as commitment to more and more adequate models of reality. The educated person is the one whose life is characterized by commitment to models worthy of shaping one's life.

We are not so much concerned or constricted to what happens in a school or classroom except insofar as it contributes to or inhibits the process of education. We are concerned that education is too often equated with the amount and breadth of skills and information one has mastered rather than the critical fidelity to adequate models that we are proposing. We will, however, make the case that not only is the acquisition of skills and information the condition of critical fidelity but that in acquiring them one can simultaneously absorb and refine the strategies of evaluation.

Commitment

The verb commit means to do something. The do-ing of commitment is twofold in this context. It is trusting the unfolding of one's existence to the interpretive patterns of a model while at the same time constantly re-evaluating the model's adequacy. Re-evaluation may result in revaluing the model so that one's faith is not simply sustained but deepened, or it may effect abandonment for a better model.

It has been said that the worst enemy of the better is the good. It is too easy to coast through life on the initial choice of a good model, like a ship going passively from lock to lock in a canal. Commitment to the better is by definition a searching fidelity. One cannot live humanly without defining interpretations of existence. When a better interpretation or explanation comes along, the wise person, the educated person, channels his or her living into these sluices.

The tentativeness with which one is called to be faithful to a model should not be confused with the paradigm of fidelity to persons. A person, any person, is an end; a model is a means. It is a means of rendering our environment and especially our personal association more fruitful. We assume as an overriding thesis that persons are the ultimate embodiment of the consummatory. Whichever model contributes to this experience of the other is a better model.

There are certain other assumptions implicit in

education considered as commitment to more and more adequate models. Among those we have detected is that models yield their value under analysis. The point can hardly be debated without resorting to analysis with all the circular reasoning that implies. Consider this alternative, however. Suppose it is not possible to distinguish any model as better than any other; then, as we mentioned in the first chapter, the choice of a model would be a matter of taste, and education would be superfluous.

Of course, the criteria for discerning the better which we propose constitute a model to be evaluated. It must undergo the application of itself to itself. Unless the criteria generate still more precise, still more comprehensive and perhaps even completely other or contradictory models of evaluation, they must be abandoned for criteria which will do so. Investment of life warrants a model that can grow with us in extension and depth.

Teaching as Proposing

Teaching is best described as the activity of proposing skills, information, and criteria for evaluating models. The term "proposing" has been carefully selected. The work or, rather, art of teaching must steer the narrow course between simple presentation and indoctrination in its manipulative sense. Proposing means literally to put forth something, but it is used in conversation in ways which convey some of the elements essential to the teaching act.

A "proposal," until the onset of government and foundation grants, was almost synonymous with an offer of marriage. That context provides some fertile analogies. A proposal of marriage usually comes at a ripening point in an on-going relationship. In other words, there is a great deal of "readiness" activity before the offer is made. In selecting "proposal," therefore, we wish to incorporate in our theory all the findings of developmental psychologists which indicate that not anything can be proposed at any time.

A perceptive suitor is also, as a good teacher should be, very careful about the aesthetic of the proposal. He chooses an appropriate time, an appropriate place, and appropriate words. The model being offered, creative co-existence, demands a life investment of such magnitude and extension that only a fool would take less care and claim to be earnest. Even when the proposal appears to be made spontaneously or on the spur of the moment, we submit that the "spur" is a kind of intuition that the relationship has sufficiently unfolded, that the moment is aesthetically appropriate.

A final element common to an offer of marriage and teaching as a proposal is the attention which must be paid to involving the entire person. The distinction between the mind and body or the cognitive and affective is a logical distinction like height and weight. The distinction may be helpful for purposes of analysis but in actuality the two never exist separately. A rule of thumb might be: the greater the life investment called forth by a model, the more the total person must be involved. Totality of involvement is essential to the movement of someone from the status of a student of physics to a physicist as well as the movement of a boyfriend to the status of a betrothed. This element could probably be best explored in a psychology of conversion.

Proposal is more commonly used today, especially in academia, to describe the attempt to secure funds for some specific purpose from a government, a corporation or a foundation. The authors of a proposal try to persuade would-be sponsors that the model they are describing is worthy of investment. It seems safe to say that a proposal of this type is never made on the spur of the moment. Great care and forethought go into the description of what is to be done, with a conscious effort to establish that the model being proposed fulfills the criteria the authors assume will be applied to it as well as competing models. The criteria might be that the model makes sense, is unique, capable of realization, makes a contribution to the whole of society, and is "cheap" at whatever the price. Proposal in this context exemplifies good teaching which entices investment in a model primarily by addressing itself to criteria.

We have also selected proposal to emphasize the point that learning is optional. Required courses, required attendance or the threat of exams cannot guarantee that learning, still less education, will occur. Learning is the incorporation of skills, information, and criteria. Education takes place in the process of their application. The more a student can enter into the construction of the proposal, the more intrinsic to the proposal is the motivation to learn; that is to say, the more organic is whatever is learned to the be-ing of the student. Attempts to motivate the student that are outside the proposal itself may indeed be the occasion of mastering skills, information and criteria, but hardly ever the occasion of education. The material is acquired but the acquisitions are accretions that overlay living instead of qualifying it. All of this is another way of saying that education is more likely to take place when an inductive method of proposing is used than when the deductive method is used.

Proposing Skills

Skills are learned powers of doing things competently. They always imply experience so that no skill is acquired or should be proposed without again taking into consideration the findings of developmental psychologists. One learns skills the way one learns anything—optionally. Teaching in the sensory-motor stage primarily takes the form of embodying a model for imitation. The proposal of an embodied model which elicits imitation remains a powerful technique in every endeavor that claims to be educational. Even in these early stages the proposal incorporates the element of enticement that exists in an offer of marriage. The imitation of walking and talking is encouraged and rewarded—in general, made to appear worthy of whatever investment it takes to acquire the skill. At this stage, however, except for the natural inclination to imitate, most of the motivation seems to come from outside the model itself in terms of what an infant can appreciate: smiles, praise, prizes.

As the child grows and becomes more adept at the skills already learned and is well into learning others, the realization that he or she is being equipped with what are basically two types of skills may begin to dawn. A child may notice that there is more than one way of handling one's food, more than one language, or that not everyone reads from left to right across a page, from the front of the book to the back. On the other hand, there are certain skills such as riding a bike or playing the violin which everyone seems to do in the same way. At whatever point a child can be asked to suggest why this might be the case, the child is prepared to begin the task of education; the child is ready to begin to evaluate how and why and whether one lives the way one ought.

It will become apparent that some skills are demonstrably the most efficient way invented to date of doing something. Others are conventions. Some are "mere" conventions, for example, the American custom of cutting one's food with a knife held in the right hand and then replacing the knife with a fork to eat the food. It is quite obviously not as efficient as the European custom. Having realized this a student may consider whether it is worth the time and the brunt of social opprobrium to learn and exercise a more efficient model. Other conventions such as language or models of reading are not so demonstrably less efficient than competing models. But a particular language or mode of reading may be the condition of communicating in one's own milieu. In sum, a student may learn that there are better ways of doing things and conclude that there are even better reasons for not doing them that way—a very sophisticated conclusion.

Proposing Information

It has become a truism that teaching is not to be confused with giving information. We submit that it is a truism that has passed too uncritically into educational lore. "Inform" means literally to give something its essence, to animate. A term with such connotations cannot be too easily dismissed.

Information considered simply as the names and the relations between things is a means of participating in the creation and extension of one's environment. Primitive peoples treated the learning of names with an acute realization of the power it conferred. The story of *Rumpelstiltskin* marvelously illustrates the power. Informed of the crafty gnome's name the beleaguered queen at once assumes possession of her identity and can begin to participate creatively in her environment. A less fanciful but no less marvelous story of our century documents the possibilities in information. Most of us are familiar with that moment in Helen Keller's *The Story of My Life* when she understands that the manual impressions on her hand name what she is experiencing: water. She continues:

I recall many incidents of the summer that followed my soul's sudden awakening. I did nothing but explore with my hands and learn the name of every object I touched; and the more I handled things and learned their names and uses, the more joyous and confident grew my sense of kinship with the rest of the world.[1]

The put-down of information derives from a

confusion of two of its species. All names and relations (information) are models of reality, as we have
been at great pains to demonstrate. But some of the
information, such as that the bases in a ballpark are
ninety feet apart, or that "Hallowed be thy name" is
the second line of the Lord's Prayer, is easily verified
or falsified. Therefore, the information is rather con-
fidently delivered. Unfortunately, the explanation or
interpretation of this data which is also information
is too often given with the same glib confidence. But
it is precisely at this point that a student can be
helped to explore the probability that we do not have
access to reality as it is. A teacher who proposes an
explanation or a number of them with the reasons
why one or another is considered more believable
than competing explanations makes a significant
contribution to the development of critical skills in a
student. Education cannot take place without information. Information is the content of our models,
the names and relationships in which we believe that
animate our existence. The critical and tentative
form in which we live this content indicates the degree to which we have been educated.

Criteria for Evaluating Models

It must be evident by now that the separation of
skills, information and criteria was done for clarifi-
cation. They do not exist separately. No skill is proposed or acquired without information. Indeed, in
most instances, information is given to promote the
acquisition, application or perfection of a skill. The
various disciplines impart information to facilitate

one's thinking historically, mathematically, philosophically, and so on. Any goal short of that does not conceive of education as a critical way of "doing" life. Similarly, the proposal of criteria should be of a piece with the proposal of skills and information as has been suggested in the sections which examined those areas. We will concentrate here on the applications of criteria.

Persons are employing criteria from their earliest years. They believe the world-view imbibed with the acquisition of language as, and probably because, it is proposed by significant persons. Early experience of competing models undoubtedly occasions some kind of rudimentary evaluation of this criterion. Confronted with the street information that there is no Santa Claus, children are forced to choose their authorities. Authority probably remains throughout our lives a compelling reason for believing. But we become much more demanding and sophisticated in our notion of who or what constitutes authority. It would be sophomoric to refuse to believe "on authority." How many among us are capable of critiquing the theory of relativity or the law of uncertainty in physics? We are right to rely on those whose competency has been demonstrated at least to the physics community.

Although we have maintained that our purpose is not to explore the criteria of any particular discipline, the process by which the members of the physics community or any field of study arrive at, evaluate, and apply criteria has more general applications in which we are interested. The process of applying criteria appears to be characterized by three moments: reflection and evaluation (both of which are communal in nature) and construction, by which we mean the personal appropriation of the hammered out criteria.

"Publish or perish" is an injunction which should not be confined to scholars. It is only in the activity of making explicit the matter of one's beliefs that one can realize what is entailed. One must have at least published one's thinking to oneself before it can become grist for reflection and evaluation. Publication for others allows the community through its questions, remarking of weaknesses and reinforcing contributions, to foster the reworking, refining and perhaps extension of the model in which one believes. Mutual criticism which intercommunication provides threshes out the nutriment from the chaff in one's commitments. Even conscience, which is usually considered inviolately private and that to which one owes ultimate and unending fidelity, comes from the Latin *com+scire*, to know together. The disciplines set up societies, conventions and journals to foster just such communal reflection. A good teacher sets up comparable structures between himself or herself and the students as well as among the students.

Earnest reflection is almost synonymous with the application of criteria or at least the sensed need for criteria to apply. The members of a discipline are quite scrupulous in winnowing out proposals whose credibilia leave something to be desired. In other words, each discipline has very well defined criteria with which to evaluate its scholars' contributions. The most creative individuals within a field, however, are probably among those who put forward theories to which standard criteria will not apply.

What frequently happens then is that the subject area is split into two schools: those who dismiss the theory by applying the old criteria and those who somehow are convinced of the theory's credibility and reflect on their conviction to discern what criteria have made the conviction possible. If the new school begins to dominate the field, the new criteria become the touchstone of credibility for subsequent theories until the next "revolution."

We are suggesting that, in the last analysis, it is not the content of any school which marks it off from other schools in a particular discipline. It is the criteria used to evaluate the model. That is, it is not so much what is believed as the reasons for believing which effects the different positions within a specific field. It is the appropriation of criteria rather than the appropriation of the material which is the crucial feature. The adherents of a particular point of view had to make their own the criteria which constitute that viewpoint as credible. In a sense they have to re-create the criteria in themselves, for themselves. Analogously, the proposal of criteria must in some way generate the students' personal construction of the criteria which must be their own and must resonate in their experience.

The educator can derive many helpful cues from the construction and application of criteria within the disciplines. Life-defining models, however, are best evaluated by aesthetic criteria.

The term "criteria" has such a cerebral connotation. It requires no little effort with students who rail against abstraction to call their attention to the fact that every word they use, with the exception of proper names, is an abstraction. What they are real-

ly taking exception to, and accurately so, is the bi-
furcation of mind and flesh. It is difficult for them to
see that a "mere" theory could energize a person's
total response. They can be helped, however, to see
that almost any term—cat, love, disaster—elicits a
bodily response. It can further be proposed to them
that since such is the case, criteria for evaluating
models must take this aspect into consideration.
Aesthetic theory moves in that direction. We have
claimed that there is no such thing as the purely cognitive, but using the term seems to emphasize and
perpetuate the distinction between the intelligible
and the sensible. The aesthetic, on the other hand,
has long been regarded as the intelligent exploration
of the sensibilities. Perhaps the best way to clarify
what we mean to include in our use of the term aesthetic is to contrast it with anesthetic. Anesthetic
connotes the suspension of reason and feeling. By
aesthetic we mean reasoned feeling or feeling reason.

When called upon to reflect on the adequacy or
inadequacy of the models in which one's life is in-
vested one may find that anesthetic criteria have
been operating more than aesthetic. The commitments may not be the result of desire and consideration so much as happenstance. One happens to be a
woman, an American, a Christian, a member of this
family. One lives out the model as one conceives it to
be defined by society, frequently unaware of the vari-
ables within the model or that other models exist.
Consciousness raising, whether we are talking about
the feminist activities of women's lib or the educational activities of Paulo Freire, constitutes tech-
niques to make us aware of just such a situation, but
since living is a processive phenomenon it is not

enough to know where we have been and where we
are. This seems to be the problem with value clarifi-
cation. After learning what one's values are, what
criteria does one use in evaluating past choices and
making new ones?

A person concludes that a life-defining model is
more adequate when it satisfies his or her questions
and talents—that is, when the life suggested by the
model offers a mode of being that makes one's experience available to oneself, not simply in a meaningful way, but in a way that suggests meaning will
accrue to one's entire life as a result of embracing
this model. It is a model through which one can
address oneself to all the loose ends of his life, gath-
ering them into a whole that enhances both the
strands and their resolution. The model must also, in
the words of the classified ads, offer advancement. It
must intimate that living out commitment to this
model will offer an increasingly novel and satisfactory mode of integrating the apparently disparate
aspects of one's life.

Such criteria can only have application to what
we have been calling life-defining models. Those are
the paradigms whose content after commitment
henceforth qualify one's entire existence. One begins
to see everything in terms of an historian, a physicist, a husband, an American. In the models cited,
however, it appears that while they may be accurately termed life-defining, they are not so extensive in
themselves to comfortably cross-reference one another. While one's love and affection for a wife may
empower an historian to do his best work, and the
story elements of his marriage may enhance fascina-
tion with his spouse, it seems that a still more com-

prehensive mythos is required which will promote an historian's work qua historian and a husband's commitment as husband. We think that such a model is best described as religious. In effect then we are suggesting that education is commitment to more and more adequate religious models.

Study Guide

1. This work describes the educated person as "the one whose life is characterized by commitment to models worthy of shaping one's life." What theory of knowledge does this statement imply?

2. The commitment spoken of in this definition is further defined as a "searching fidelity." Does our conversational use of the word "commitment" (e.g., commitment to a cause, to a principle, to a vocation) usually have this active connotation?

3. What might distinguish a man with a dynamic, active commitment to justice from one who sees commitment as adherence to a fixed principle?

4. Commitment involves here not merely trusting oneself to a model but constantly re-evaluating that model's adequacy. How in this context might fixed adherence to a cause prevent a person from being truly faithful to it?

5. Teaching is described here as the activity of pro-

posing "skills, information, and criteria for evaluating models." On what grounds do the authors
compare "teaching" with a "proposal"?

6. In the search for more and more adequate models
we eventually commit ourselves to modes of interpretation which can define our life. How has
the choice of a career qualified your manner of
interpreting reality?

7. Life-defining models must be evaluated in terms
of their ability to satisfy the whole person, to
offer a mode of being that makes one's experience
available to oneself—not simply in a meaningful
way, but in a way that suggests that meaning will
accrue to one's entire life as a result of embracing
this model. Would any of the life-defining models
in this chapter be adequately life-defining (historian, physicist, husband, American)?

8. Why must the criteria for evaluating life-defining
models be aesthetic (involving feeling as well as
reason, "reasoned feeling" or "feeling reason")?

9. The model to which one commits oneself must
promise advancement and "offer an increasingly
novel and satisfactory mode of integrating the apparently disparate aspects of one's life." Consider
one of the life-defining choices you have made.
Were you aware of it as a challenge and means of
integrating life more fully?

Readings

On the structure of education see:

Bruner, Jerome S. *The Process of Education.* New York: Vintage Books, 1963.

For further reading in educational theory see:

Dewey, John. *Democracy and Education.* New York: The Macmillan Co., 1916.
Rogers, Carl. *Freedom To Learn.* Columbus: Charles E. Merrill Publishing Co., 1969.

On developmental theory see:

Erikson, Erik. *Childhood and Society.* New York: Norton, 1950.
Goldman, Ronald. *Readiness for Religion.* New York: Seabury Press, 1970.
_____. *Religious Thinking from Childhood to Adolescence.* New York: Seabury Press, 1968.
Piaget, Jean. *The Growth of Logical Thinking from Childhood to Adolescence.* New York: Basic Books, 1968.

Note

1. Helen Keller, *The Story of My Life* (New York: Doubleday, Page & Co., 1922), p. 37.

3
A Case for Orthodoxy

Models, as we have limited their use, obviously not only permit change: the best models promote it. Perhaps, one should more accurately say, they promote development. Most of us, however, at least initially, do not make the distinction that development is a species of change. We react to the difference. Any change is more or less difficult for some of us. But most have learned not only to live with change, in some cases we seek it. We have become used to changing theories in science. If we were to read on the front page of tomorrow's newspaper that a majority of scientists had concluded that not the sun but some hitherto unseen body was the center of our system there would be nothing to resemble the reactions to Galileo's support of the Copernican theory. Our "hmmmmm" might easily be followed by turning to the TV section to note the night's movies.

On the other hand, we can be most interested in the latest models that a consensus of the medical community poses. Should they conclude that a particular drug once considered beneficial for heart disorders is now determined to be of no use or even detrimental, we might receive that news with a more emotional response. We have then come to live with the vagaries of science and the reinterpretations of history, economics and literature. We have even learned to accept a lowered pitcher's mound, extended leagues and the experiment with designated hitters in baseball. The single area in which change or development has been and remains most resisted is religion.

In this chapter we hope to demonstrate by a brief overview of the Judaeo-Christian tradition that of all the sectors of life religion is that which most congenially reflects the theory of knowledge outlined in Chapter 1.

Orthodoxy and the Jews

Interestingly enough, "orthodox" literally means straight or right *opinion*. *Doxa* was considered in Plato's discussion of knowing either conjecture or belief as opposed to *episteme* (knowledge) which was a grasp of reality as it truly is. The literal use of the term orthodoxy, therefore, is quite consonant with the notion of models as we have developed it. All we have to work with *are* opinions, conjectures, beliefs. How could it be otherwise? Religion refers to a relationship (*re*: back; *ligare*: to bind). The terms of the relationship have historically been appraised to be the person or community and God.

Historians and sociologists sometimes cite religion as the particular contribution of the Jews to our civilization. We suggest that this is the case because they proposed a model of God that became a criterion for what constitutes "religious."

The Greek philosopher Xenophanes had employed an insightful touchstone to explain his ridicule of the Olympic gods: *theoprotes*, "that which fits the divine." Yet centuries before the Jews had recognized such a criterion as an elemental component of their relationship with the deities. God was not to be imaged, not to be named (Ex. 20:1-7, Deut. 5:6-11). It was this boundless concept of God that allowed the Jews to evolve the sophisticated notions of monotheism and omnipresence. It was also their dominating theology of a God who cannot be contained within genus and species definitions that allowed them to be freely anthropomorphic in discussions of God's relations with the descendants of Abraham.

We must thematize. We must speak. The perfect tribute will not remain silent. The difficulty always lies in confusing the word with its referent. The construction of the golden calf illustrates the idolatrous nature of this confusion (Ex. 32:1-34). The brazen serpent, on the other hand, is healing because it is seen as a manifestation of God's power but not God (Nm. 21:6-9). Similarly, the Jews are able to consider all the psalms as prayers although they are addressed to oneself, one's friends, enemies, all of nature and God. God is not equated with any or all of these objects. Not even God. Had not God, when pressed for a name, answered, "I am who I am"? Hebrew scholars tell us that this should be interpreted not as the ground for a theory of God as being, but as the much more homely, "Mind your own business!" God is that on which one cannot get a "fix."

Orthodoxy and Christianity

Christianity preserves, reinforces and extends the Judaic intuition of a model of God that is beyond representation. The Christ himself commits nothing to the permanency of writing (the single instance in John's story of the woman taken in adultery where Jesus writes on the ground is an interpolation not found in any early MSS). The followers of Jesus who later record the oral tradition do so in four different versions. One might read G. B. Shaw's introduction to his *Androcles and the Lion* to see what contradictions an unbelieving fact-seeking person derives from the Gospels.

Those who reject Jesus as the Messiah are described as those who have a defined, petrified model of he who is to come. "We all know where he comes from but when the Christ comes we will not know where he comes from" (Jn. 7:27). These people have forgotten the lesson that the use of the tetragrammaton (YHWH) was inspired to inculcate. To us it now appears as an amalgam of consonants, which aptly signifies an incomprehensible deity—a deity who must be imaged because we are an imaging species but who refuses to be confined to our images or constricted to our expectations.

Those who persist even today in reading a formula for behavior from the Gospels are still in the position of imposing a fixed model where none exists. For example, if one reads Jesus as a model of non-violence one must be embarrassed by the activities of Jesus among the money changers of the temple, particularly as they are detailed in the second chapter of John. The violent imposition of religious opinions is considered especially reprehensible today.

Early Doctrinal Development

The inconclusiveness of the Good News permitted the most extraordinary development of dogma, once again promoting and advancing the insights of the tetragrammaton. The heresies of Christianity have always been attempts to eliminate the irreconcilables of the central doctrines. Heresies always make much better "sense" than the finally hammered out dogmatic statements. The Arian and Docetist theses, that Jesus was less than God or that God only appeared as man, would have removed a number of problems that are only compounded in the attempt of professed monotheists to articulate a model of a triune God.

Perhaps the difficulties are best exemplified in an historical account of the Nicene Creed. The Nicene Creed promulgated by the Council of Nicea (325) concluded: "But as for those who say . . . that the Son of God is of a different hypostasis or ousia . . . these the Catholic Church anathemizes." You will recall that we now profess that there *are* three different hypostases but one substance in the Godhead. You might also notice that hypostasis is the exact Greek equivalent of the Latin *substantia*. What the Fathers of the Church resorted to was, in effect, saying that hypostasis shall not mean what it in fact did mean—substance—and that therefore there are three hypostases but only one substance in the deity. Because we can so easily verbalize "There are three persons sharing one divine nature," we too often miss the incomprehensibility of our profession. Either we are talking about what is beyond our experience or language to handle or we are not talking about God. In any case, what the doctrine of the Trinity essentially does is to explode even the neatness of our monotheistic notions of God.

So too with the pronouncements of Chalcedon.

It seems that certainly one is on the right track when one conceives of God as the absolutely Other. When the participants of the Chalcedon Council insist on defining the person of Jesus as true God and true man, what they actually do is to say that even this most appropriate designation—"God as Other"—will not contain God.

Similarly, Nestorius proposed the reasonable compromise that Mary be ambiguously called the Mother of Jesus. The Council of Ephesus, we might think rather blasphemously, counterpropounded that she is the Mother of God.

Unfortunately, most of these central pronouncements of the Church are referred to as definitions. That is precisely what they are not. Definitions are the imposition of boundaries. Everytime one comes across a piece of furniture upon which one can sit, one can call it a chair. What the "definitions" of the early Church did was to make it impossible to locate any boundaries or string any net of logic in which one could "catch" God. The so-called definitions of the Councils are closer to "the sound of one hand clapping" of the koans than they are to definitions. It is in this sense that they are appropriate models of God—dynamic because they incorporate contradictions, the kind of conflict that is literally fruitful beyond the capacity of any one age or all ages to imagine.

The Theology of the Middle Ages

The distinction between the two dominating schools of theology in the Middle Ages seems captured in Bernard's assessment of Abelard: "The trouble with Abelard is that he does not see as in a glass, darkly." The Schools have sometimes been characterized as the neo-Platonists vs. the Aristotelians, or the Franciscans vs. the Dominicans. For our purposes we will distinguish those who emphasized negative theology—God is not this, nor this, nor this—from the theologians best exemplified in Thomas Aquinas who seems by the sheer weight of his output to be saying God is this, this and this. But when you consider what he is saying—God's essence is existence, that is, indeterminate being, and the careful elucidation of his use of analogy, one realizes that his "We know God as unknown" is a summary of his corpus, not a condemnation of it.

Analogy is the attempt to come to grips with the dilemma of our need to thematize, to say something, and the recognition of the ineffectualness of speaking about the ineffable; it is the strained resistance to the equally tempting options of idolatry and pure agnosticism. Ironically, the strain is most apparent when analogy works with less and less inappropriate models. That is to say, the less inappropriate a model is, the more likely it is to be considered hard information about God. For example, it is probably more appropriate to call God "Father" than "Cabbage," but then it becomes difficult to remember that God is not Father, nor this, nor this. In sum, we are suggesting that the theologies of the Middle Ages advanced the theological enterprise to the extent that they refined and honed concepts that maintained the model of a God which cannot be conceptualized.

The formulae of the Counter-Reformation the-

ology manuals seem to undermine the thesis that we
have been proposing, namely that doctrines are
models whose religious quality is best demonstrated
by their open-endedness. We would submit, on the
contrary, however, that the Post-Tridentine—pre-
Vatican II—era of Roman Catholicism negatively
validates our point. The stagnation and lack of theological development in this period of Catholicism un-
derscores Whitehead's observation: "The progress of
religion is defined by the denunciation of gods. The
keynote of idolatry is contentment with the prevalent
gods."[1] On the other hand, the very fracturing of the
Christian Church which forced sects to define and
defend conflicting positions constituted a physical
embodiment of the complementaries, contraries and
contradictions that in today's ecumenical climate appear to be the source of such a revitalization and
resurgence of Christian thinking.

Evaluating Models

Religious orthodoxy as traced in our brief and
undoubtedly simplistic overview of the Judaeo-Christian tradition also fulfills the criteria for evaluating
competing models which we began to detail in the
previous chapter.
    A model derives its validity from its capacity to
interpret experience in a way that extends the coherence of our existence. This might be called the consummatory element of the criteria we are proposing.
It is that aspect of a model which calls forth the
response, "So that's what it is. Of course!"—our
"Eureka." The more extensive the context in which

this interpretation allows us to function, the greater awe with which we pronounce our Eureka. A classic, someone has said, is a work whose most fruitful years are ahead of it. While this obviously applies to works of art as a criteria, it is equally valuable in the choice of scientific or even moral models.

Euclidean geometry is a good model to work from to build a house, but non-Euclidean geometries are an advance because, while not denying the proposals of Euclidean geometry, they enable us to build space stations beyond our planet.

Among medical theories a drug that not only eliminated a disease's symptoms but kept side effects to a minimum would be a better drug than one which simply did the former. A drug which eliminated the disease, had no side effects and, moreover, contributed to the overall well-being of the patient would be a better drug yet.

Similarly with moral models. Situation ethics as described by Joseph Fletcher has been criticized not because the position he propounds is immoral or amoral. As a matter of fact, it reads something like Thomas Aquinas' development of the virtue of prudence. It has been criticized because the "situation" of the title is not comprehensive enough. The injunction to speak the truth is an example of a "better" moral model. While in a particular set of circumstances deception may appear to be beneficial, such an interpretation cannot take us too far. As one begins to extend its application, one must undermine the intelligibility and trust on which any society is grounded. It would be as if one synthesized a drug that could only treat one disease in one person. There would be no point in mentioning such a drug in medical school; it has no further application.

An artful poem or painting, on the other hand, by its illumination of an individual moment or experience not only crystallizes and formulates the artist's and the reader's or viewer's experience which is the consummatory, "Yes, that's it," but the degree of its aesthetic quality is contingent upon the degree of its ability to suggest that all one's experience is material for artistic crystallization; that we are members of a larger community than we can even imagine; that our identity can be constituted by insightful constructs of past peoples and cultures and, by extension, future peoples and cultures. Great art, therefore, is the prime example of models which not only elicit a Eureka but enable us to function with this interpretation in a context that is no less than the total human community. We are suggesting that to the degree a model in any discipline approximates great art, it is, to that degree, a better model than its competition. One more reasonably believes the better model.

It must become obvious that as the illuminative and extensive qualities of models become deeper and wider, they will include and resolve more and more contraries and contradictions. The best models will suggest even more than they can resolve. Nicholas of Cusa criticized the scholastic endeavor because it was based on the principle of non-contradiction: a thing cannot be and not be at the same time. Quantum physics suggests that the fifteenth-century Nicholas was on to something. It is precisely the incorporation of contradictions that accounts for the magnitude of the context in which contemporary physics is fruitful.

When one examines models that are simply constructs of absolute contradictions, and then one compounds the contradictions by insisting that in some way the models are not simply the verbalizing of the mutually exclusive, one is dealing with models that not only express the best interpretation of one's own existence but the extension breaks the bounds of all conceivable limits. While such a model includes the aesthetic extension to the whole of the human community, even the whole of the universe, it transcends these conceivable entities and locates us in a context we have come to call religious. Our response to such models is not Eureka but worship.

In the Judaeo-Christian tradition we find such religious models: an imageless, unnameable God, *a triune* God, a God-man, a Mother of God. The final personal test of a model, however, is its fruitfulness in our own lives. Does it make it possible for us to both generate and accept still other explosions of God being God? We will now explore a contemporary model of God that appears to meet the criteria we have proposed.

Study Guide

1. The best models promote change. We expect change in all areas of life but resist it in the area of religion. Why is fixed adherence to religious definitions inconsistent with Orthodoxy in its literal sense?

2. This work contends that the Jews contributed to

civilization by proposing a model of God that became a criterion for what constitutes "religious." How can the concept of God as "beyond representation" be more important than any "beliefs" which they passed on? How can this model of God be considered a "criterion"?

3. Christianity preserves, reinforces and extends the Judaic intuition of a model of God that is beyond representation. Mention several ways in which the Gospels are inconclusive and contradictory.

4. Early doctrinal development further preserved the Church from fixed adherence to a particular notion of God. In what sense do the authors consider the early definitions of the Church to be dynamic?

5. The theologies of the Middle Ages contributed to theological progress to the extent that "they refined and honed concepts that maintained a model of God that cannot be conceptualized." How do the authors envision the conflicting religious schools as furthering theology?

6. In what way does religious orthodoxy fulfill the criteria for evaluating models? How does the experience of contradictions locate us in a new context?

Readings

On models and religion, see:

Barbour, Ian G. *Myths, Models and Paradigms.* New York: Harper and Row, 1975.

For studies of the development of dogmas, see:

Dulles, Avery. *The Survival of Dogma.* New York: Doubleday & Co., 1971.
Pelikan, Jaroslav. *The Emergence of Catholic Thought.* Chicago: University of Chicago Press, 1971, pp. 100-600.

Note

1. Alfred North Whitehead, *Adventures of Ideas* (New York: Mentor, 1955), p. 18.

4

A Contemporary
Model of God

This chapter will propose to show that process theology offers fresh perspectives and new resources to present a model of reality in a way that harmonizes with contemporary experience and the twentieth-century world-view. Indeed, we suggest that the processive framework is the most appropriate contemporary embodiment of the insights explored so far and has become perhaps the most genuine theological option for the Christian religion.

The real question in philosophical theology is whether theological thinking stands up under criticism; whether it provides a coherent account of the facts, which may be validated, in some fashion or other, by its logical consistency and by its capacity to account for the data which experience provides. One of the tasks of this chapter is to show that process theology does in fact meet these criteria. In addition, we will suggest other lines of thought that are not fully developed. As such, they cannot be criticized as though they represented fully articulated positions, but they are worth mentioning for the purpose of indicating the great variety of implications of "process" for some classical problems of Western religious thought.

Situating the Problem

Nothing is more offensive to the present generation and nothing is more useless to the theological enterprise than the maintenance of a system of abstractly defined truths which bears neither examination in nor relation to the real world in which we seem to exist. The Greek metaphysical presentation of theology has become irrelevant for the modern world because a metaphysical theology that looks at truths in an immutable and universal way cannot properly grasp and present unique historical events precisely as unique and historical.

Reflecting on faith is a continuing task; formulations are never finished. The world of today is sufficiently different from that of the past to cause a need for radical reformulations. Too frequently, official religion no longer answers questions of daily life in a form that many can understand and affirm by and in their own experience. Many traditional ways of formulating the Christian faith, whether these are from Catholic or Protestant sources, do not seem to speak meaningfully to many people, yet somehow these same people feel that the Christian faith itself is or might be meaningful. Especially in recent years, with a growing secularization of culture, but with an increasing awareness that human beings require some sense of purpose and direction if their lives are to be more than trivial and inane, there is a yearning for some presentation of Christian faith which will both reflect the historical emphases of the Christian tradition and be alert to contemporary experience. Clearly, the critical theological situation of today is characterized by a continuous tension between reorientation and conservatism, between renewal of faith and loss of faith. People are afraid of losing the stabilities of bygone days, but are equally afraid of suffering a loss in their existential commitment to today's world. Many have become hesitant and doubting believers, straddling their way in a kind of borderland Christianity.

The Process Model

In an earlier chapter, we touched upon the shift in the scientific world-view from Newtonian mechanism to twentieth-century science. Converging with the notion of evolution, the influence of the scientific revolution gained considerable momentum from the thought of Alfred North Whitehead, whose work attempted to elaborate a metaphysics that would be consistent with the new science. Thus was born American process theology.

Process theologians hold that advance in thought is no longer possible within the framework of seventeenth-century cosmology of the three-tiered universe. They suggest that the fundamental need of our time is a reorganization of basic cosmological schemes of ideas, and so they have gone to the evolutionary categories of the modern world as a possible framework for philosophical and theological formulations. The reason for this shift is that theology, philosophy and science all co-exist in a large cultural matrix. Not only do their imagery and concepts interact among themselves and shape our experience in a given period of history, but our experience itself is undergoing radical change. Out of this change, new

metaphors are being formed. And it is this broad
cultural transformation which forms the context for
the development of process theology.

The central theme in the process model is the
doctrine of God and his relation to the world. In the
final chapter of his major work, *Process and Reality*,
Whitehead criticizes three notions of God: that of
the ruling monarch in the likeness of Caesar, the
ruthless moralist of the Hebrew prophets, and the unmoved mover of Aristotle. Instead, he presents God
as unbounded Love, the poet of the universe, our
fellow sufferer, who understands. There have since
been numerous attempts by other process thinkers to
expound, extend and explicate Whitehead's theories,
to reconcile them with Christianity wherever possible, and to critique the Christian theological tradition—especially Thomas Aquinas and the classical
theism he represents—which separates God and the
world. This split results from the Greek idea of perfection and Aristotle's concept of relation. Aristotle
views relation as involving change and dependence
and hence imperfection. He concluded, and the Tho-
mists with him, that the world can be related to God
because it is dependent on him, but God cannot be
really related to the world. If he were, then he would
be dependent on creation and would not be the unmoved mover required by the Greek idea of perfection. This image of an aloof and distant deity is not
consistent with what Whitehead calls "the Galilean
origins of Christianity."

The Nature of God in the Process Model

The Bible speaks of the living God; it sees him

as intimately related to every aspect of creaturely existence both in nature and history, and the world is "open" to him and his activity upon it. The conception of the deity which process thinkers espouse is that of its being dipolar: God has a *primordial* and a *consequent* nature. As *primordial*, God is the ground of actuality, or, in other words, God is the source of all possibilities, the condition for everything that is. The second aspect of God's nature is *consequent* upon the creative advance of the world. In the *consequent* nature the world reacts upon God. The world passes into God's *consequent* nature where its values are made available for the on-going process of reality. In this aspect, the possibilities which are eternal and abstract are actualized by God. To put it another way, God has an *abstract, absolute* aspect and a *concrete, relative* aspect. In the former aspect are contained myriad possibilities, and it is in this sense that God can be referred to as primordial deity. In the latter aspect, God is self-surpassing creativity; he is eminently social and relative. God is in the world and the world in him; he receives into himself what occurs in the world so that it becomes an occasion for ever new and richer possibilities and concretions. This is conveyed by the term "pan-entheism," which is frequently used by process thinkers to express the interpenetration of God and the world while at the same time not identifying God with the world. Its meaning can best be illustrated by an example from human experience.

Our own relation to our bodies is but an image of God's relation to the "world." While we may have a heightened awareness of some "part" of our body such as when we experience an excruciating toothache, splitting headache, or some injury to an arm or leg, we do not identify our being-ness with our tooth, hand, arm or leg. We are more. Similarly, when we find ourselves immersed in our work, we do not identify ourselves with our work. We are more than what we do. So, in a sense, as the human self is related to its body, God is related to the world.

The process model of God then is *societal*, of which one member is preeminent but not absolute. In this model the universe is pictured as a community of interacting beings, rather than as a monarchy. God possesses the greatest conceivable degree of real relatedness to all others and is for that reason the most truly absolute that any mind can conceive. By this is meant that only God is really related to everything. God's sphere of interaction is the whole universe and his relation with all beings is unsurpassingly immediate and direct. This fact becomes glaringly apparent when we reflect on our ability to relate to others. No matter how "open" our personality and how deeply and freely receptive and responsive we are to others, we are effectively related to only a few others during our lifetime. We realize that although we may study history and anthropology, we can never be related to the billions of selves who lived before us or will come after us. This is not true of God. Instead of being merely the barren Absolute, which by definition can be really related to nothing, God is in truth related to all others. God's being related to other beings is itself relative to nothing beyond God himself. It is human nature to be related finitely; it is God's nature to be related infinitely. Thus, God is the supremely related one. God is the poet of the world, with tender patience leading it by his vision of truth, beauty and goodness.[1] The love in

the world passes into God and floods back into the
world. God is concerned with the world and is involved in its suffering and its tragedy. The world,
man, and human events make a difference to him.
The deepest reality of God is revealed not in his de-
tachment or in his power, but in his love.

Certainly, the notion of an infinitely related
God is not one readily accepted by conventional
Christianity. The assertion that God is both himself
and yet endlessly related poses no small problem at
first glance. It is only in the process framework that
the problem of the co-existence and co-agency of the
infinite and the finite, the necessary and the contingent, the eternal and the temporal, the absolute and
the relative can be resolved.

The God of the process model is living, active,
constantly creative, infinitely related, and ceaselessly
operative, and movement, dynamism and activity are
central to the universe. Neither God nor the world
reaches static completion, but both are involved in
change, and change involves the emergence of real
novelty.

Some Comparisons

It is already apparent that many of the criteria
we proposed in the preceding chapters are met by the
process model as we have described it thus far. Let
us recall these criteria, briefly suggest how they are
met by the process thinkers, and then isolate one for
greater in-depth analysis.

(a) *The most profound models incorporate contradictions; they do not impose boundaries.*

As we have pointed out in this chapter, process theologians do not define God. In their schema, God is intrinsically two-sided, at once supremely relative and supremely absolute. This is so because his being related to all others is itself relative to nothing.

Process theologians are quick to point out that while it is true that many of the so-called metaphysical attributes of God ascribed by traditional Christianity primarily did attempt to refuse limiting God to the specifically human categories of finitude, they in fact ended up being nothing more than negative statements which do no more than pay metaphysical compliments to God.

That the process model employs contradictions and thereby imposes no boundaries can best be summarized by Whitehead's famous antitheses:

It is as true to say that God is permanent and the World fluent, as that the World is permanent and God is fluent.

It is as true to say that God is the one and the World is many, as to say that the World is one and God many.

It is as true to say that in comparison with the World, God is actual eminently, as that, in comparison with God, the World is actual eminently.

It is as true to say that the World is immanent in God, as that God is immanent in the world.

It is as true today that God transcends the World, as that the World creates God.[2]

(b) *Models, as we have limited their use in the*

preceding chapters, obviously not only permit change; the best models promote development.

One of the basic views of the process thinkers is that the deepest Reality is not static but dynamic. In the process model, change is a positive factor in experience and not a negative one. Contrary to the Greek ideal and medieval Christianity, change, when intelligent and responsible, like all perfections should be applied to God. Even when Whitehead proceeded to examine the nature of God from the standpoint of the metaphysical, he exclaimed, "God is not to be treated as an exception to all metaphysical principles, invoked to save their collapse. He is their chief exemplification."[3]

(c) *A model derives its validity from its capacity to interpret experience in a way that extends the coherence of our existence.* Process theology takes seriously the existentialist analysis of subjective human experience which deals with interpersonal relations, memory, human freedom, the relatedness and temporality of human beings, and all uses of these to illuminate the nature of God and his relation to the world. This task is considered essential to redeem existence from triviality and futility. In Whitehead's words:

> . . . our existence is more than a succession of bare facts. We live in a common world of mutual adjustment, of intelligible relations, of valuations, of zest after purposes, of joy and grief, of interest concentrated on self, of interest directed beyond self, of short-time and long-time failures or successes, of different layers of feeling, life-weariness and of life-zest.[4]

We have suggested earlier that the degree of aesthetic quality for a model is contingent upon its ability to suggest that all of one's experience is material for artistic crystallization. We have also suggested in the preceding chapter that we are members of a larger community than we can even imagine, and that our identity can be constituted by insightful constructs of past peoples and cultures, and, by extension, future peoples and cultures.

Common to all process thinkers is the conviction that life is more than useless passion. All of life is taken seriously, including feelings, apprehensions, intuitions, poetic insights, and the like. Whitehead pointed out that the beauty of the world, the depth of reality of the world, and the value of the world in its whole and in its parts are all bound together by the fact that the universe exhibits a creativity with infinite freedom, and a realm of forms with infinite possibilities.

These notions are consistent with the process model because it is societal in nature. Although one member is pre-eminent in it, the universe is pictured as a community of interacting beings. Reality is social because a plurality of centers of activity is envisaged. There is reciprocal interaction, giving and receiving, in the community of being, and God has a unique and direct relationship to each member within this community.

In the process model, our identity is constituted by history. Every event is novel action—the joint product of past causes, divine purposes, and the emerging entity's own activity. John Cobb, for example, sees God as the pre-eminent person in a community of interacting beings. His writings develop the pluralism and personalism of the process model. In history, mankind can grow in the coherent articulation of human experience. Norman Pittenger's works demonstrate that each succeeding generation adds its own insights, its distinctive apprehension to the growing body of experience:

> It is for each generation to allow the tradition to come alive in its own experience; to see that it is handed on, purified and given contemporary significance, with such modifications as may be required; and then to hand it on to the next age, for the enrichment of those who follow.[5]

Thus, history is seen as the coming alive to the present generation of the past which has shaped it.

(d) *The best models will suggest even more than they can resolve.*

As we suggested in the very first chapter, the most significant models will be characterized by the unpredictable, the spontaneous, the not yet formulable and the ineffable. They will also be instrumental in that they will suggest, even as they stand, the possible generation of more nuanced, more comprehensive models. Central to the thinking of the proponents of the process model is the recognition that the realities of any experience are to be accounted deeper than man's powers of observation and description. This is not to imply the rejection of reason and observation, but to acknowledge their limitations, and to recognize that the structures of reason which we are able to formulate and employ are but tentative ventures in apprehending the meaning of those realities. As such, they are not definitive and final descriptions of them.

Translated into process categories, this means that God influences each becoming occasion, which differs from that entertained by the previous human experience, and seeks to "lure" it beyond the mere repetition of past purposes and past feelings or new combinations among them. God is thus at once the source of novelty and the lure to finer and richer actualizations embodying the source of novelty—the one who calls us beyond all that we have become to what we might be. In such a conceptualization, God is fundamentally understood as he who calls us to ever-greater love, life and freedom.

Similarly, in the process model, God is not thought of as utterly unchangeable and empty of all temporal distinctions. Rather, he, too, is understood to be continually in process of self-creation, synthesizing in each new moment of his experience the whole of achieved actuality with the plentitude of possibility as yet unrealized. Yet he never determines the outcome of any moment and never violates the self-creation of each being; God respects the order of creation.

Since there is no completed set of actual things that make up the universe, creativity is conditioned by the actual world relative to each novel coming-to-be of individual actual entities in the temporal world. Thus, we may at last render really intelligible the deep conviction that it is our own secular decisions and finite processes of creative becoming which are the very stuff of the "really real" and so themselves somehow of permanent significance. Because God is most immediately affected by all that we are and do, the future for which we ultimately live our lives is the unending future of God's own creative becoming, in which we are all given to share.

Our main point in this chapter is to underscore the contrast of the process model with traditional doctrines that have insisted only on the permanence, unity, eminent actuality, transcendence, and creative power of God. All of these we affirm, but only in polar tension with other factors usually negated of God. John Cobb sums it up succinctly for us when he says:

. . . the Creator-Lord of history is not the all-determinative cause of the course of natural and historical events, but a lover of the world who calls it ever beyond what it has attained by affirming life, novelty, consciousness and freedom again and again. The Lawgiver is not the source of arbitrary, imposed rules, established once and for all from on high, but the establisher of ever-new possibilities of righteousness which both destroy and fulfill generalizations based upon the past. The Judge is not one who, at some future date, will reward and punish in accordance with our obedience but the one who can give us only what we will receive, thereby rewarding the responsive with new and richer challenges but "punishing" the unresponsive by the poverty of their new possibilities. The Holy One is not the primordial sacred which transcends and annihilates all separateness and individuality through mysterious and dehumanizing cults, but the immanent-transcendent Ground of life and creativity which calls us ever forward in and through the ordinary events of daily life and the often terrifying occurrences of human history.[6]

In the following chapter, we will attempt to suggest that if the final, personal test of a model is its fruitfulness in our own lives, then the process model offers inexhaustible possibilities for our growth in becoming more human.

Study Guide

1. How do the authors characterize the theological situation today? Give examples of the "continuous tension between reorientation and conservatism." Would you also describe the position of many today as "straddling their way in a kind of borderland Christianity"? Explain.

2. What is the central theme of the process model? Why is it important that a contemporary model help us deal with this facet of reality?

3. How does the nature of God as presented in the process model conform with the biblical revelation of the "living God"?

4. What is meant by God's "primordial" and "consequent" nature?

5. In what way is the process model "societal"?

6. In what ways does process theology present us with "a more profound model" according to the criteria described in preceding chapters?

Readings

On the affirmation of the world and its relation to God, see:

Cobb, John B., Jr. *God and the World*. Philadelphia: Westminster Press, 1969.

For a general orientation into the central issues and the major thinkers of process theology, see:

Cousins, Ewert H. (ed.) *Process Theology*. New York: Newman Press, 1971

For an introduction to the doctrine of God in a process framework, see:

Pittenger, W. Norman. *God in Process*. London: SCM Press, 1967.

Notes

1. Alfred North Whitehead, *Process and Reality* (New York: Macmillan, 1929), p. 526.

2. *Ibid.*, p. 528.

3. *Ibid.*, p. 521.

4. *Religion in the Making* (New York: Macmillan Co., 1926). p. 77.

5. Norman Pittenger, *God in Process* (London: SCM Press, 1967), p. 85.

6. John B. Cobb, Jr., *God and the World* (Philadelphia: Westminister Press, 1969), pp. 65-66.

5
Life as Creative Response-Ability

While we would agree with Whitehead that abstract speculation has been the salvation of the world —speculation which made systems and then transcended them, speculations which ventured to the furthest limit of abstraction—we propose that *a final, personal test of a model is its effectiveness in our personal lives*. That is, we suggest that the test of any speculative theory, theology or belief system is how it affects practice, how it affects the quality and style of our living, or, to put it another way, the difference it makes in the rest of our lives.

In this chapter we will attempt to illustrate how the process model would affect one's personal life by considering four areas central to Christian living: the Incarnation, faith, worship and engagement.

Incarnation

Although the Christian doctrine of the Incarnation does in fact favor the dynamic and relational view common throughout history it was most often interpreted in static terms and subordinated to the notion of God as unmoved mover and timeless absolute. In the process view, however, God is *ever* incarnating himself in his creation. This means that he is ever entering into it—not as if he were absent from it and intervened in it now and again, but in the deeper sense that he who is unexhausted in himself ever "informs" all creation, expressing himself more and more fully, until the whole created order becomes, in some sense, "the body of God."[1]

Jesus is not an intrusion from outside but the decisive instance of God's creative, loving presence in the world. He is the climactic and definitive point for God's presence in the world. And here is a pivotal point: the human life of Jesus not only reveals divine activity at work in his person, although it does that, but it is also revelatory of God's activity in the whole cosmos. Jesus is the clue to the rest of God's creative activity. The relationship with God intended for all humankind is actualized in Jesus. He is the classical instance in whom the human race is shown what it can become. In this view of the Incarnation's meaning, therefore, all of humankind takes on new significance. Every person matters; no one is without value. Each human being makes a difference always and all ways.

The process framework makes it possible to affirm the divinity of Jesus without contradicting his full humanity. This task of affirmation is a perennial one and such an attempt is necessarily but an "essay" in reconception which itself is in process, while making no pretense to being conclusive or exhaustive. So for the process thinkers the Incarnation and all "incarnations" become opportunities for thinking through once again what it means, if one is a Christian, to confess that Jesus Christ is Lord, to the glory of God the Father.

The Meaning of Faith

What does faith mean to a Christian in the process framework? Faith in the process framework is faith as we have been describing it in the human framework. In a specifically religious sense it means that rather than possessing "the faith," one is engaged in the process of "faith-ing." Within such a stance, one thing becomes immediately apparent about theologizing on faith. Diverse visions of reality are strengthened by the excellence of the theologies to which they give birth. Thus, theologizing on faith is a continuous business, and because it is one cannot claim to possess any exact verbal formulations of it. Theology, as well as philosophy, is an eternal beginning, which on the one hand carries with it an absence of certainty, while on the other hand affirms with it a trust and commitment. Paradoxically, in process thought, it is this position which conveys the optimistic conviction that nothing is in vain, even though there are no guaranteed beliefs. For the process thinker, then, faith is much more than assent to propositions or dogmas; it is itself a living process, a faith-ing. It is not fixed, but dynamic, always moving and developing. The Christian understands faith as a continual challenge to grow in responsibility and to surpass one's self. Faith-ing means never to arrive, but always to ask the further questions: What more can I do? How better can I love?

To "faith" is to be serious about life, to recognize that all that happens in life really matters because it matters to the eminently related one—God. It is this conviction that becomes one's ground of confidence, and it is in this sense that we have suggested that faith is the fundamental category of existence.

Such a position encourages a stance of reverence for life and its mysteries. It means that we recognize that no dogma or belief is so sacred, so final, so absolute that it is above rethinking, reinterpretation, or restatement. And in fact we accept the possibility that this recognition might, even more painfully, necessitate abandonment of previously held dogmas or beliefs.

The process model then acknowledges limitations of all conceptual categories and the finitude of every human statement. To "faith" today is to be aware of and accept the tentativeness of each interpretation of belief in its uncontrollable aspects. It is to live in the tensions between unshakable confidence in life and its deepest reality, and the futile attempt to achieve an all-encompassing view of the world. It means living in half-finished houses with many things left unsaid because they are, at least for the present moment, unsayable.[2]

Worship

To be truly religious is to be truly worldly—and this in the sense that we become more religious as we respond ever more appropriately to life and its meaning in the world. The only proper response to such a realization and experience of reality is worship. Prayer is personal worship—personal response to our encounter with reality.

In the process view, our prayers are limitless in their effectiveness, but always in us and through us and never by means which are contrary to the order of creation nor in violation of human freedom. Prayers are never a means of informing God about events, needs, or desires he would otherwise know nothing about; they are not an exchange of information. Nor are they a means of coercing God to do what he otherwise would not do. Prayer is more than petition or intercession. It is the aligning of our desires with the great cosmic desire for good which is God himself. Prayer is the internal and attentive identification of our feeble human willing, purposing and aspiring with God's loving care and activity. Through prayer we are purified; our prayers of petition and intercession are attempts to recognize our real needs. The emphasis in prayers and intercession is on our part—we do not supply what is lacking in God. So too, in a love relationship between two persons communication is necessary. Even though one party may already know what is disturbing the other, or what the other feels, or what the other needs, yet the word needs to be spoken. We must communicate. It is through prayer that we are opened up to God's presence and care, that is, his grace, in our life. But even in this sense prayer would have no meaning unless God were really affected by it. This is borne out by our own personal experience. If we stop and think about it, we can recall instances when we prayed as if our prayers really did affect God. Although most of us have outgrown our childish attempts to make God an offer he can't refuse, yet in our moments of deepest grief, and exuberant joy, we still pray as though we do affect God.

As we have pointed out elsewhere, the process model is societal by its very nature. For this reason,

the central act of Christian worship throughout the
ages, the Eucharist, takes on renewed significance
within the process framework. The societal, communal aspect of worship is epitomized in the Eucharis-
tic celebration. Eucharist is a two-way gift—God's
giving of himself in Jesus, and the giving of persons
to God and to each other. We are societal and we
need to pray together because we need the deliberate
awareness of God's presence, power, and love which
worship makes available to us. In the process view,
then, worship is essential to Christian life.

Engagement as Building the Earth

Once we admit that the fundamental fact of our
experience is process, the meaning of "engagement"
in life has the most portentous ramifications. Our
creation in the image of God is a call to participate
in creativity, in all of its splendor and suffering. It is
a call to become responsible for doing all that must
be done to make the world a more human place in
which to live, one which reflects more fully the glory
of its source. Our task is everywhere and needs no
state of completion. This is so because in the process
view the love of God is love of the one whose boundaries to life are not defined by a final state of affairs,
but by ever new possibilities of growth and development.

In the process model, there is a circular movement from the world to God and from God to the
world. Since the powers of human knowledge are
limited, and God is without limit, this process has no
end. So too, the goal of building the earth is not to

achieve the peace of completion but the peace of openness to new experience in a shared community.

Our vision of what is ultimately real and valuable develops gradually. Each notion gains new dimensions as various interrelations are worked out. The world is not a mere object, not an "it," but it is always the world of existing persons, a world of "thou's." This anthropocentric world "becomes" through what happens to it in historical deeds, and consequently it represents alternate possibilities of development. As long as there are persons there will be novelty.

The world is not regarded as a fixed framework of uniform occurrence as was presented by the Greek concept but the dynamic site of an ever new creative order of life which becomes ever richer, ever filling with new meaning and quality. Life becomes the very process of interaction between humans and the world, that inclusive and continuing dialogue whose emergent meaning depends on how intelligently we respond to the world's action upon us. Human development is radically this-worldly. It does not lie somewhere beyond the boundaries of everyday life but must be sought within them, and it consists in the integrity, harmony, coherence—what we have called the aesthetic quality—of the very process which is life.

Not only does God influence every occasion of experience: he is in turn affected by each experience. He takes up into himself the whole richness of each experience and provides the ultimate justification for our giving of ourselves fully and freely to the tasks of human experience: to knowing and doing, feeling and loving, with all of their sorrows and joys. Thus even miseries and failures count in the business of life.

God enables each person's life itself to make a difference—to contribute not only to the life of others, but also to God's own lasting life, to which each life makes a real difference.

Our increasing ability to engage in life is important because life is a project to be achieved in time and through history. Together we can strive for those societal conditions which would make possible our free response to God. Once we become aware of God's call to share in creative activity, we begin to grow in the consciousness of our duty to make that response possible. We begin to realize that we have both the power and the responsibility to reconstruct our world, reshape our lives, and create new options for the future. To be able to do all of these, the risks of freedom must be taken together with all of the possibilities of its misuse. To be sure, our own past does influence us in the future, but it does not necessarily prevent our progress, even though it can slow us down in becoming more fully human. Through all of our stumblings and wanderings, we always remain free and therefore responsible. In our own life history, we can see that much good has been accomplished however slowly and reluctantly. More things have gone well than have gone awry. Good wins out, not in a cumulative evolution toward a climax, but through waxing and waning in myriad ways. This in fact has always been the orthodox position of Christianity from its earliest beginnings: Jesus Christ has conquered suffering and death; through him we are brought to new life.

For process thinkers, engagement is the response we make to the meaning of reality, and its meaning cannot be found until we have merged our own interest with that of the universe. Decision-making, concern, commitment and belonging—all of these determine authenticity in human life, and all require that we engage ourselves in scientific, technological, social, political, and economic activities. Thus, the interrelatedness of pertinent aspects of modern culture with the humanization process is affirmed by the process model. A world in process is one that experiences itself in its non-divinity, a world that presents itself to humankind as the building-site and laboratory of all people everywhere. This world does not exist in a pre-established order from which an eternal order of things can be read, but it is a world which is coming into being as a result of human action, in the process of directed scientific and technological planning and social and political revolutions. Process theology suggests that the Christian's attitude toward engagement should be one in which the world is seen not so much to be consecrated, captured, or given meaning and salvific relevance, but rather to be recognized, endorsed, and brought to fulfillment.

In summary then, we suggest that if we are asking whether God's existence can be reconciled with our deepened experience of ourselves as free co-creators of the world, the processive approach with its notion of God's persuasive personal action in the world, and confirmation of such reconciliation with stress on its mutuality, offers pathways for yet further development. If we today are asking whether God's existence can be accepted without destroying our dignity in our free creative role in the universe, the processive approach with its unwillingness to make God an exception to metaphysics, with its rejection of God as a despotic ruler of the universe, and with its view that we and God are the responsible co-creators of the universe, shows that we are not forced to choose between our dignity and God's existence. If we are asking, in other words, how the process model affects our personal lives, we can see that it offers challenges and invitations which can radically change our whole lives. The material we dealt with in this chapter is in no sense an adequate description of the complexity of how process thought can affect our personal lives. It is only a beginning. But we are convinced that the process model, as we have presented it thus far, fulfills the aesthetic criteria described in the first chapter to such a degree that it can properly be called "religious." How one educates to such a model will now be our concern.

Study Guide

1. The authors propose that "a final, personal test of a model is its effectiveness in our personal lives." In what particular areas do you believe faith should make a difference in a Christian's life?

2. In what way does the process theology interpretation of the Incarnation differ from that which dominated Christian thought in the past? How does this shift in perspective affect our view of the

created order, the person and humankind, the person of Jesus?

3. What does "faith" mean to the Christian according to process framework?

   A. What is the relationship of faith to "doing" and "loving"?

   B. Why does faith involve acknowledgment of the "tentativeness of each interpretation of beliefs"?

4. What is the significance of worship and prayer in the process framework? How does the "societal" nature of the process model affect one's understanding of the Eucharist?

5. How does the notion of experience as a process affect the quality of one's engagement in earthly tasks? Are we still influenced by the Greek concept that the world is a fixed framework of uniform occurrence? How does the process model promote vitality and enthusiasm in engagement?

6. How does the process model help us to reconcile God's existence with our "deepened understanding of ourselves as co-creators of the world"?

Readings

On God in secular experience, see:

Baum, Gregory. *Man Becoming*. New York: Herder and Herder, 1971.

For a statement on Whitehead's God and the world, see:

Whitehead, Alfred North. *Process and Reality*. New York: Macmillan and Co., 1929.

For a comprehensive interpretation of the significance of process thinking for Christian faith, see:

Pittenger, Norman C. *Process Thought and Christian Faith*. New York: Macmillan and Co., 1968.

On the spiritual life in the process framework, see:

Pittenger, W. Norman. *Trying To Be a Christian*. Philadelphia: Pilgrim Press, 1972.

Notes

1. Pittenger, *op. cit.*, pp. 19-20.
2. William Hamilton, *New Essence of Christianity* (New York: Association Press, 1966), p. 14.

6
Teaching as Proposing Within a Processive Model

In the processive perspective, education is not the imparting of static content but is a vital process of growth. It does not involve only verbal, abstract, conceptualized thinking, but rather it includes a depth of interiority that is self-reflective, that is dynamic, creative and intensified by interpersonal relations. Hence, as such, education can never take place in isolation from community and passionate fidelity to a life-long process of inquiry.

We have tried to make the case that not only is the acquisition of skills and information the condition of critical fidelity but that in acquiring them one can simultaneously absorb and refine the strategies of evaluation. It is on this very point that narrow approaches to religious education have failed. For example, the traditional, classical approach, perhaps most aptly exemplified in Catholic circles by the Baltimore Catechism, was information-centered. The accretion of information and skills necessary to acquire it became ends in themselves, while the technical collection of doctrinal statements supported a deductive approach to education.

Concentration upon information is an inadequate approach to education because it is based on the misconception that there is a context which is separable from a way of living and communicating with others. That is why proponents of this approach in religious education circles failed; they did not recognize that salvation, however it may be conceived, must be a human reality or at least decipherable in the context of human reality.

The information-centered approach is similar to the elementalist psychology movement of the 1920's. Its basic idea was to take what the children were to learn, break it down into small pieces, and then teach these pieces bit by bit with the hope that once they received all the bits the children would be able to grasp the whole. History was quick to reveal that while the children did learn the elements, they had no idea what they meant when they had learned all the bits. The sum of the parts did not equal the whole. As might be expected in a field which had and still has no theoretical base, the children taught in this manner did not become mathematicians, historians, physicists or the like. We suggest that in the parallel narrow approach to religious education, children who were given all the facts or bits of information were incapable of putting them all together. No matter how carefully the pieces were broken down, children did not reach religious maturity simply by completing carefully defined courses of study.

In the last quarter century, an attempt was made to move one step beyond the traditional informational approach in religious education. As theorists in other disciplines were moving more and more toward inductive, individual-centered learning, the so-called kerygmatic approach was born in Catholic circles. Now, instead of showing the way to approach the task, the Bible and the liturgy were used as the new content. Under a new guise, the old aim still dominated: the purpose of religious education is to produce acceptable behavior. And the best way to accomplish this end is by supplying the students in the last analysis with the right formulas.

So too with the more recent "life-centered" or "experience-centered" approaches—they demonstrate that taking a non-directive approach with the old vision increases the gap and the problem: one must change one's vision—one's model—if one is serious about effecting more and more adequate religious education. Failure to do so results in obscurantism—the refusal to speculate freely on the limits of the traditional methods. Of course this danger is not peculiar to Catholic religious education. A look at the history of liberal Protestantism will reveal that "Christian education" has many parallels to the examples just cited. In fact, all of these approaches are currently operating side by side in both Catholic and Protestant circles.

Proposing as Growth

The kaleidoscopically changing world demands a questioning, inquiring, evidence-based attitude and "content" presented in new ways. It means questioning established educational practice. In other words, religious education must be reborn from the intersection of good educational theory and sound theological study.[1] This attitude, this vision, is most comprehensively embraced by the process model we have been proposing in previous chapters.

Earlier we suggested that education takes place in the application of skills, information and criteria, and that the critical and tentative form in which we live the content of our own models indicates the degree to which we have been educated. This becomes all the more apparent when we realize that the present generation has deeper insights into human nature than any previous generation; it has access to information that no other generation has had. In the process model we are suggesting, education is for life and the enhancement of life.[2] For that reason, all of the information proposed by teachers must serve the life process. If it does not, then it is cluttering the curriculum. In such a framework, tradition takes on a new significance, for it is seen as the coming alive of the past to the present. It calls for a willingness to continually draw upon the cumulative experience of mankind, not simply to confirm what has been achieved but to bring forth a richer quality of life and to make this life more widely accessible. Tradition is regarded more as a dynamic of clues or hints from which we attend to ever novel aspects of ever evolving reality. This calls for relational thinking and life-long learning, which is best met by the process model.

We have also suggested earlier that commitment to the better is by definition a searching fidelity. This is especially true in religious education. The quest for precise definition and comprehensive doctrinal statements does little more than short-circuit the search process. Whitehead claimed that premature precision is deadening to religion. Religious education must be a continuing search engaged in by the whole community to actively promote human growth in diverse ways.

One does not have to be a seer to admit that the world is changing at an exponential rate. If religious education is to meet the challenge of the dizzying changes in science, technology, communications, and social relationships, religious educators cannot rest on *answers* provided in the past, but must put their trust in the *processes* by which new problems are met.

Thus one of the main educational goals must be to develop individuals who are open to change and who can live more comfortably with change than with rigidity. It follows that in a processive framework, religious education must necessarily be increasingly ecumenical, capable of dealing with the full spectrum of human concern—in Comenius' phrase, to educate all men to full humanity. We are suggesting that a processive religious model, a life-defining model, will require that teachers reconvince themselves of the importance of self-criticism, and that they construe the critical approach as both *process* and *product*.

A climate of criticism could then be created that would be self-reinforcing and would affect the entire field of religious education by encouraging its critical integrity. Such critical reflection is integral to any educational model which would call itself religious. Dewey has made it very clear that experience *per se* has little value educationally without reflection, which produces the understandings, the interpretation, the foresight, and the means of control of experience and its effects.

Criteria for Evaluating Religious Models

Religious growth is dependent upon all other growth. The first criterion of a religious model is how well it is attentive to the qualitative differences of the learners. How does it respect the limits of the learner's abilities as revealed by developmental psychology? How does it take into account intellectual maturity, linguistic limitations and restrictions of experience?

Another criterion for evaluating religious models would be their continuing capacity to deliver and fertilize our experience. In an earlier chapter, we demonstrated that for process thinkers God acts by evoking response, while respecting our integrity. This response and its correlative ability to integrate disparate aspects of life to increasingly novel and satisfactory modes distinguish the adequacy of competing religious models. It is interesting to note that there has been much written on the role of reward and punishment in learning, but very little indeed on the role of interest and the lure of discovery.[3] It was Albert Einstein who remarked that it is in fact nothing short of a miracle that the modern methods of instruction have not entirely strangled the holy curiosity of inquiry. In the process framework, one of the main purposes of education is to provide situations which will restore, stimulate and enhance the unquenchable curiosity which the student had as a small child.

A given moment of experience, a given configuration of occasions, can illuminate what has gone on before its appearance or emergence, can enter into peculiarly intimate relationships with what surrounds it and with which it has connections, influencing and perhaps being influenced by those occasions, and can open the way for novel, perhaps surprising, developments in the future.[4] In the presence of the model the teacher acts as one who lures, not pushes, who motivates, not coerces. The teacher is like a neutron by whose action is initiated a chain reaction of creative transformation. The teacher serves as a sponsor, allowing for the waxing and waning of the students, fostering, nurturing, sustaining them in their endeavors, always trusting in the process of education.

The model suggests that a sound approach to education is grounded in the structure and dynamism of the cosmos itself. We also maintain that basic to every teaching/learning situation is the assumption that at some point the students will not only achieve autonomy to consciously confront their already accepted frames of reference, but that they will be able to be transformed by the experience. This, needless to say, is more easily asserted than accomplished, but if we didn't think it were so, then education as we have described it would be superfluous.

To deny that it is possible to educate toward more and more adequate models is to assume either one of two things: that we are born with an innate knowledge that would make any and all education unnecessary, or that we are all partners adrift in the sea of ignorance. If education challenges the principles by which an individual lives, each reorientation to reality may indeed shake an individual's very foundations. That is why the final test of a person's life is the quality of communal life one nourishes. This is what we mean when we suggest that education is commitment to more and more adequate religious models. In this sense, of course, religious education does not differ from any other kind of good education. Its distinctiveness can only lie in the complex reality of a faith-ing community. But this much we do assert: the person committed to the process model of God is an exemplification of all the criteria we have set up for an educated person. The truly educated person is a truly religious person.

Epilogue

We have attempted to present a model, not a strategy, to point a direction rather than describe a reality. We do not presume that the conceptual scheme presented here is the final answer. In particular, we have no predictions to make, no program and clear-cut prescriptions for the future of religious education other than this: the extent to which those concerned with religious education are prepared to refine and expand their theological and educational vision may well determine the adequacy with which the challenges of our own age and that of the future will be met.

Study Guide

1. Why, in the context of this work, is it important that students acquire skills and information? Why must religious educators avoid exclusive concentration on this approach?

2. Why is it necessary to change one's vision—one's model—if one is serious about religious education?

3. Why should a religious model take into account the qualitative differences of learners? How does the presence of a more profound religious model help a teacher "lure" her students toward discovery?

4. What relationship between religious education and the students' experiences is proposed here?

5. Explain the following statements:

   A. ". . . the final test of a person's life is the quality of communal life one nourishes."

   B. ". . . the truly educated person is a truly religious person "

6. Central to any successful religious education is the teachers' "ability to refine and expand their theological and educational vision." Would such teachers be purely theoretical and speculative? Give examples. How might the presence of the process model affect practical decisions on the conduct of a religion class?

Notes

1. Gabriel Moran, *Design for Religion* (New York: Herder and Herder, 1970), p. 19.

2. Norman Pittenger, "Process Theology and Christian Education," *Religious Education*, Vol. LXVII, no. 3, May-June 1973, p. 311.

3. Jerome Bruner, *The Process of Education* (New York: Vintage Books, 1963), p. 50.

4. Norman Pittenger, *Alfred North Whitehead* (Richmond: John Knox Press, 1969), p. 24.